NATURAL DISASTER ZONE
EARTHQUAKES AND TSUNAMIS

BEN HUBBARD

FRANKLIN WATTS
LONDON • SYDNEY

Franklin Watts
First published in Great Britain in 2019 by The Watts Publishing Group

Credits
Editor: Elise Short
Illustration and Design: Collaborate Agency

Picture credits:
Shutterstock : Eky Studio: cover, 1; seksan wangkeeree : cover, 1;
Chirokung: 9; Peter Hermes Furian : 9; Breck P. Kent: 10;
Visual Intermezzo: 12

HB ISBN 978 1 4451 6590 5
PB ISBN 978 1 4451 6591 2

Printed in Dubai

MIX
Paper from
responsible sources
FSC
www.fsc.org
FSC® C104740

Franklin Watts
An imprint of
Hachette Children's Group
Part of The Watts Publishing Group
Carmelite House
50 Victoria Embankment
London EC4Y 0DZ

An Hachette UK Company
www.hachette.co.uk
www.franklinwatts.co.uk

CONTENTS

INTRODUCING EARTHQUAKES AND TSUNAMIS

Earthquakes and tsunamis are deadly natural disasters that bring widespread destruction to people and property. They can demolish cities, wash away villages and swallow whole coastlines. They are violent, powerful and virtually impossible to predict or prevent. So what are these natural disasters?

WHAT ARE EARTHQUAKES AND TSUNAMIS?

An earthquake is a sudden, extreme shaking which can crack open the ground and reduce entire cities to rubble. A tsunami is a massive wave, or series of waves, which can reach 13 storeys high and sweep away everything in an unstoppable wall of seawater.

Together, earthquakes and tsunamis have killed millions of people and created some of the greatest catastrophes in history.

EARTHQUAKE FAST FACTS

- Ninety per cent of earthquakes occur along the Ring of Fire (see page 9) around the Pacific Ocean.

- An earthquake's shaking is made by seismic waves which are triggered by movement in Earth's tectonic plates (see pages 8–9).

- Every year there are around 500,000 earthquakes that can be detected by scientific instruments; about 100,000 of these can be felt by people and around 100 cause damage.

- The largest recorded earthquake was a magnitude 9.5 in Bio Bio, Chile in 1960.

TSUNAMI FAST FACTS

- Tsunamis are mainly caused by earthquakes, but also by landslides and underwater volcanoes.

- Tsunamis are sometimes called 'tidal waves', but they have no connection with the tides.

- In deep water, tsunamis can travel at speeds of over 800 kph.

- Tsunami waves are often only around 30 cm high in deep water, but can reach over 40 m by the time they hit the shore.

WHEN AN EARTHQUAKE STRIKES

On 12 January 2010, a massive magnitude 7 (see page 13) earthquake struck the Caribbean island of Haiti. The earthquake flattened buildings, blocked roads with debris and destroyed the island's electricity and water supplies. Haiti's capital, Port-au-Prince, was the worst affected area. Thousands became trapped in the rubble or were killed as buildings collapsed.

USA

CUBA

MEXICO

Port-au-Prince, HAITI

EMERGENCY SEARCH

Soon after the main earthquake struck Haiti at 4.53 pm, violent aftershocks of magnitudes 5.9 and 5.5 followed. Many of the island's badly constructed buildings simply disintegrated under the strain. Great mountains of rubble then blocked roads, preventing emergency teams from getting their equipment through. Digging for survivors lasted for two weeks before the search was called off.

THE HUMAN COST

The Haiti earthquake left over one million people instantly homeless and destroyed the island's vital infrastructure, such as telephone lines, water and electricity supplies. Most of the island's hospitals were also destroyed, leaving many people to die from their injuries. As morgues became overrun, bodies piled up in the street. Disease followed, as did looting and other crimes.

Meanwhile, it took many days for aid and emergency supplies to get to people in need. The earthquake's death toll was estimated to be between 220,000 and 300,000, although many bodies were never found.

UNSTABLE BOUNDARIES

The 2010 earthquake's epicentre was 25 km west of Port-au-Prince, where the majority of Haiti's people live. This was not the first high-magnitude earthquake to hit Haiti. The previous large earthquake struck in 1984. It measured magnitude 8 and left 19 million cubic metres of rubble to be cleared away.

The island is prone to this kind of disturbance because it lies on the highly unstable boundary between the Caribbean and North American tectonic plates (see pages 8–9).

FASTER DISASTER FACTS

- The earthquake immediately displaced over 1.5 million people and left over 300,000 injured.

- Many foreigners pledged money to the Haiti earthquake fund using their mobile phones. It is estimated that Haiti received over USD$9 billion in donations.

- Years later, many buildings in Port-au-Prince have still not been rebuilt and thousands of people live in makeshift shanty towns in the suburbs.

A WORLD OF PLATES

The Earth's surface, or crust, is covered with massive slabs of rock called tectonic plates. These slabs are constantly moving. They move slowly, at only a few centimetres a year. But when two plates grind past each other they send out violent waves of energy through the ground. These seismic waves are known to us as earthquakes.

TECTONIC PLATES

Earth's tectonic plates move at different speeds, in different directions. The areas where plates meet are known as plate boundaries. There are three different types of boundary, where plates either push together, pull apart or slide sideways past each other.

CONSTRUCTIVE BOUNDARIES

Plates move apart and new areas of rock and magma (molten rock) move in to fill the gap. Earthquakes often occur as a result.

DESTRUCTIVE BOUNDARY

One plate moves over another, pushing it down into the Earth's mantle where its edges melt into magma. This causes earthquakes and volcanoes.

TRANSFORM BOUNDARIES

Plates trying to slide past each other become caught and stick together. As they continue to move, the plates suddenly jolt apart, which causes violent earthquakes.

EURASIAN
PLATE

NORTH AMERICAN
PLATE

Ring of Fire

PACIFIC PLATE

FILIPINO
PLATE

Pacific Ocean

INDO-AUSTRALIAN PLATE

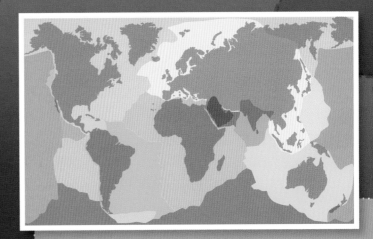

THE EARTH'S LAYERS

The Earth is made up of three main layers: the core, mantle and crust. It is made up of the tectonic plates. The crust is the Earth's thinnest layer and varies in thickness from 5 km to 80 km.

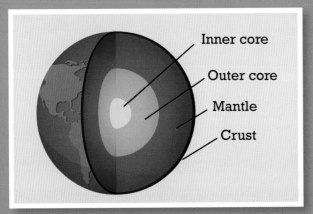

Inner core

Outer core

Mantle

Crust

MOVING PLATES

The Earth has seven main tectonic plates and around 13 smaller ones. Most of the world's earthquakes occur in the Ring of Fire, a 40,000 km zone running around the edge of the Pacific Ocean. This is where the plate boundary of the Pacific Plate meets several other plates.

WHAT'S IN AN EARTHQUAKE?

The movement of the Earth's tectonic plates causes a massive amount of energy to build up at their boundaries. When this energy is released, blocks of rock slide past each other and a large crack appears in the ground. This is called a fault. An earthquake starts deep inside the central part of a fault, called the focus.

TYPES OF FAULT

There are three types of fault: strike-slip, normal and thrust. In each type of fault, large blocks of rock slide past each other in a different way.

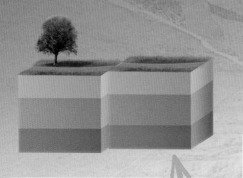

A THRUST FAULT

It is like a normal fault in reverse, with one block moving down and the other up. These often take place at destructive plate boundaries (see page 8).

A NORMAL FAULT

One block of rock moves up and the other down. These often take place at constructive plate boundaries (see page 8).

A STRIKE-SLIP FAULT

Blocks of rock slide past each other in opposite directions. These often occur at transform plate boundaries (see page 8).

ANATOMY OF AN EARTHQUAKE

When tectonic plates suddenly release built-up energy at a fault, an earthquake occurs. This is what happens:

SAN ANDREAS FAULT

The San Andreas fault is a 1,200 km long strike-slip fault on the boundary between the Pacific and North American plates. It is famous for a 1906 earthquake which destroyed the nearby city of San Francisco in the US and claimed 3,000 lives. Experts predict a large earthquake on the San Andreas fault in the future could result in many thousands of deaths along the heavily populated Californian coast.

1 The energy is released at a point inside the fault called the focus, around 5–15 km under the ground.

3 The seismic waves reach their maximum intensity at the point directly above the focus, called the epicentre.

4 Seismic waves felt on the ground can last for a few seconds to a few minutes and bring a great range of different intensities.

2 The focus releases seismic waves that travel at different speeds in all directions.

SEISMIC SHOCKWAVES

The energy released by an earthquake travels in seismic waves that shake the ground and cause the damage. The first to arrive are P-waves. P-waves travel quickly along the surface of the ground, like ripples on water. Following the P-waves are S-waves, which travel deep underground. They are slower than P-waves, but far more destructive.

P-WAVES

P or 'primary' waves can travel through rock and liquid at speeds of up to 8 km per second. P-waves are the first to be felt and shake the ground in the same direction they are moving. This can cause the ground to buckle and crack.

S-WAVES

S or 'secondary' waves are up to 1.7 times slower than P-waves, but cause more damage when they arrive. S-waves cannot pass through liquid and shake the ground at a right angle to the way they are travelling. This causes the ground to shake up, down and sideways.

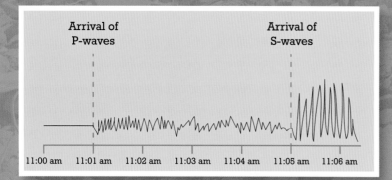

Arrival of P-waves   Arrival of S-waves

11:00 am   11:01 am   11:02 am   11:03 am   11:04 am   11:05 am   11:06 am

SEISMOMETERS

Seismometers are the instruments used to measure an earthquake's seismic waves. This information is then recorded in a seismogram. The strength of an earthquake is described by the Moment Magnitude Scale.

MOMENT MAGNITUDE SCALE

The Moment Magnitude Scale measures the magnitude of an earthquake based on readings of seismic waves. Each increase of one on the scale is equivalent to a tenfold increase in energy. An earthquake of magnitude 3 is therefore ten times more powerful than one of magnitude 2.

MAGNITUDE	EFFECTS	IMAGE
2	Not felt by people but detected by seismometers	
3	Minor earthquake felt by some people	
4	Light earthquake with some items falling off shelves	
5	Moderate earthquake with some damage to property	
6	Strong earthquake with damage to property	
7	Major earthquake with large damage and loss of life	
8	Great earthquake with severe loss of life and widespread damage	
9	Largest-recorded earthquake with whole cities destroyed and massive loss of life	
10	The effects of a magnitude 10 are not known, as one has never been recorded	?

CASE STUDY: KATHMANDU, 2015

On 25 April 2015, a magnitude 7.8 earthquake struck near the city of Kathmandu, Nepal. Nepal's deadliest natural disaster in 80 years, the earthquake killed over 9,000 people, injured 22,000 and destroyed over 600,000 buildings. Over 3.5 million people were left homeless.

PAKISTAN

Kathmandu, NEPAL

INDIA

Long Shocks

The earthquake struck just before noon, with a shallow focus 15 km below the ground. This caused the initial shock to move quickly and with great force.

Less than 50 minutes later, two aftershocks with magnitudes of 6.6 and 6.7 struck the already badly damaged area. Over the next 24 hours, over thirty-eight aftershocks caused even more damage. On 12 May, a 7.3 aftershock killed 100 people and injured 1,900.

The Human Cost

In Nepal's capital, Kathmandu, the earthquake demolished bridges, buildings and roads. Some people were killed instantly and many more were trapped under rubble. The quake also caused avalanches in the country's Himalayan mountains, killing 21 people on Mount Everest.

Reaching victims in remote villages was difficult because of landslides triggered by the earthquake. Millions of the country's earthquake survivors were instantly plunged into extreme poverty creating a humanitarian crisis.

Faster Disaster Facts

- The Kathmandu earthquakes and aftershocks were caused by an extreme thrust fault (see page 10).

- The fault line lay along the length of the Himalayan mountains on the boundary between the Eurasian and Indo-Australian plates.

- It took two weeks for rescuers to reach all of the villages affected by the earthquake.

Lasting After Effects

Many earthquake survivors lost not only family members, but also their homes and livelihoods. More than half of Nepal's schools were destroyed, meaning that nearly 1 million children could no longer be educated.

In Kathmandu, many survivors refused to re-enter their homes for fear of collapse. They erected 'tent cities' in the streets. This hampered the clean-up and rebuilding efforts.

PREDICTING EARTHQUAKES

Many of the world's largest cities lie in earthquake-prone regions. It is only a matter of time before one of these experiences an earthquake measuring magnitude 8 or more. When it strikes, such an earthquake could demolish the entire city. Predicting 'the big one' could therefore prevent great loss of life.

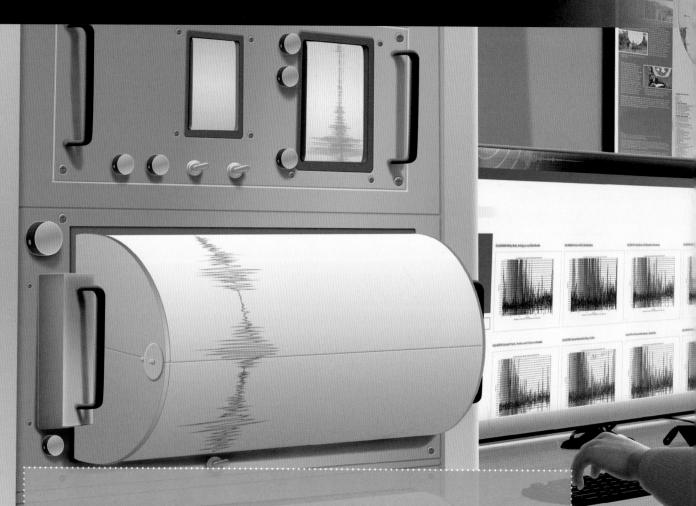

POSSIBLE PREDICTION

It is impossible to predict the time, place and magnitude of an earthquake. This is because earthquakes are created by complex geological movements many kilometres underground.

The best scientists can do is study recent seismic activity in an earthquake-prone region. They then compare this information with previous records. This can help predict an earthquake occurring within a certain time period. However, this time period can sometimes be as vague as between 1 and 300 years.

EARLY WARNING

The best way of saving lives is to warn people that an earthquake has begun. Earthquake monitoring stations work by picking up an earthquake's P-waves (see page 12) and broadcasting an earthquake warning on TV, radio and the Internet. This can give people a chance to take shelter before the S-waves arrive.

The Global Seismographic Network is an organisation with 150 monitoring stations around the world. These stations keep in constant touch via satellite and use state-of-the-art sensors to monitor seismic activity globally.

CAN TOADS TELL?

Many people believe that some animals know when an earthquake is about to strike. A study found that 96 per cent of male toads had abandoned their breeding ground in L'Aquila, Italy just days before an earthquake struck in 2009. Some researchers think that toads have a biological early-warning system that we don't yet understand.

When a Tsunami Strikes

On 26 December 2004 a magnitude 9.1 earthquake caused a massive rupture on the Indian Ocean seabed, near the Indonesian island of Sumatra. The rupture was around 1,000 km long and pushed up trillions of tonnes of rock. This triggered a tsunami with over 20,000 times the energy of an atomic bomb. It would be the deadliest tsunami in modern history.

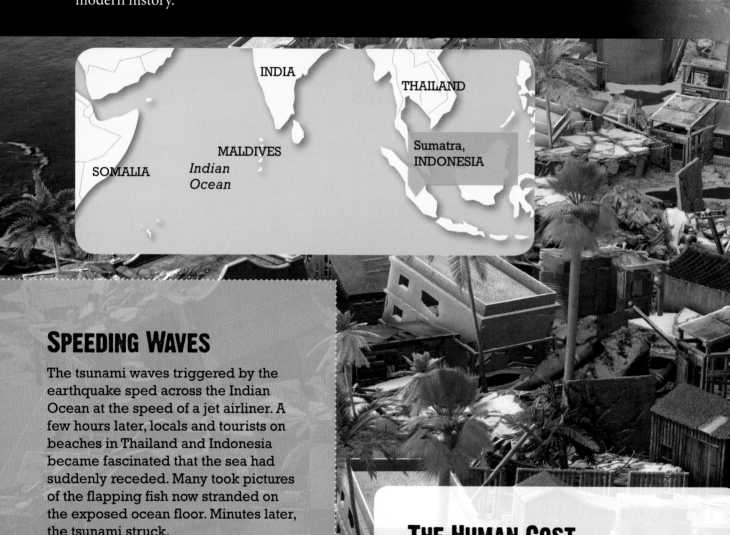

INDIA

THAILAND

MALDIVES

Sumatra,
INDONESIA

SOMALIA   *Indian Ocean*

Speeding Waves

The tsunami waves triggered by the earthquake sped across the Indian Ocean at the speed of a jet airliner. A few hours later, locals and tourists on beaches in Thailand and Indonesia became fascinated that the sea had suddenly receded. Many took pictures of the flapping fish now stranded on the exposed ocean floor. Minutes later, the tsunami struck.

In Sumatra, the waves reached 30 m in height and swept 4 km inland across the island. Within hours, the tsunami had slammed into the coastlines of 13 Indian Ocean countries, from the Maldives to Somalia.

The Human Cost

The tsunami waves demolished countless buildings and villages, drowned people on beaches and in their homes, and snatched others out to sea. By the end, the death toll reached over 230,000, with tens of thousands missing and over two million homeless.

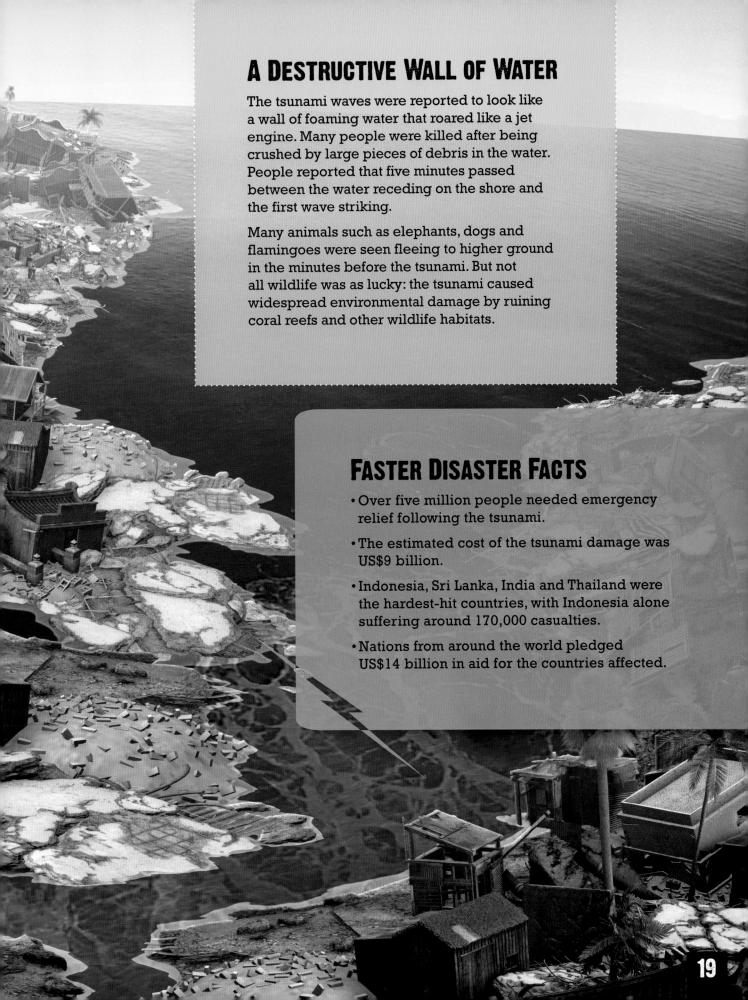

A Destructive Wall of Water

The tsunami waves were reported to look like a wall of foaming water that roared like a jet engine. Many people were killed after being crushed by large pieces of debris in the water. People reported that five minutes passed between the water receding on the shore and the first wave striking.

Many animals such as elephants, dogs and flamingoes were seen fleeing to higher ground in the minutes before the tsunami. But not all wildlife was as lucky: the tsunami caused widespread environmental damage by ruining coral reefs and other wildlife habitats.

Faster Disaster Facts

- Over five million people needed emergency relief following the tsunami.

- The estimated cost of the tsunami damage was US$9 billion.

- Indonesia, Sri Lanka, India and Thailand were the hardest-hit countries, with Indonesia alone suffering around 170,000 casualties.

- Nations from around the world pledged US$14 billion in aid for the countries affected.

19

WHAT'S IN A TSUNAMI?

In the deep oceans tsunami waves do not increase much in height, but they are fast. Tsunamis are not the same as normal waves, which are created on the surface of the water by wind. Instead, tsunamis form under water, often after an earthquake occurs on the sea floor.

TSUNAMI FORMING

During a tsunami, a great amount of water is suddenly displaced. The water then pulses up and outwards and turns into waves. The following stages show how this happens:

2

A mass of water is displaced and pushed up and outwards.

1

An earthquake or other event (see page 21) shakes the ocean floor, sometimes thrusting up a chunk of rock.

4

The water is sucked back from the coast and feeds the approaching tsunami.

3

Like the ripples caused by a pebble on a lake, waves rush out in all directions.

5

As the waves reach the coast, they become slower, higher and closer together.

20

WATCH THE WAVES

As tsunami waves reach the shore they not only become higher, but also more powerful as the water piles up behind. The water on the coast is then sucked back, exposing the sea bed.

Then a series of tsunami waves, called a 'wave train', strikes. The force of a tsunami wave can smash villages like matchsticks, sweep along vehicles and houses like they are toys, and travel for up to 16 km inland.

OTHER CAUSES

Earthquakes are not the only things to cause tsunamis. A landslide from a coastal cliff can also force a large tsunami wave to radiate outwards. Underwater volcanoes and asteroids from space can also trigger tsunamis. Around 2.5 million years ago, an asteroid named Eltanin crashed into Earth and caused a mega-tsunami that swept over large parts of South America and Antarctica.

CASE STUDY: JAPAN, 2011

On 11 March 2011, a powerful 9.0 magnitude earthquake occurred under the sea northeast of Japan. Only 30 minutes later, a series of waves measuring up to 10 m high struck the Japanese coast. The waves swept away vehicles, smashed through buildings and cut major highways in two.

CHINA

Honshu, JAPAN

Pacific Ocean

THE HUMAN COST

Directly after the earthquake hit at 2.46 p.m, Japanese tsunami alerts were reported on emergency news broadcasts and texted to people's phones.

However thousands were caught out by the waves, which destroyed whole towns as they travelled for up to 10 km inland. It is estimated 15,894 people lost their lives during the disaster, many of whom drowned in the fast-moving, debris-strewn waters.

NUCLEAR MELTDOWN

As the tsunami struck the Japanese island of Honshu, it flooded the Fukushima Daiichi Nuclear Power Plant. This cut off the plant's electricity supply and vital cooling systems, causing a nuclear meltdown in its reactor. As radioactive material leaked into the air and surrounding water, 185,000 people living in a 20-km radius of the plant were evacuated.

A COSTLY DISASTER

The Japan earthquake and tsunami of 2011 was the costliest natural disaster in history. Its effects included more than 2,500 missing people and an estimated total cost of over US$ 235 billion.

Up to 4.4 million Japanese households lost their electricity supply and 1.5 million households lost their water supply. The scale of destruction was huge: 120,000 buildings were destroyed and over one million more were damaged.

FASTER DISASTER FACTS

- The earthquake's epicentre was located 70 km east of Japan and 30 km below the Pacific Ocean floor. The shaking lasted for six minutes.
- Several further days of aftershocks were experienced, some reaching 7.2 on the Moment Magnitude Scale.
- The tsunami waves travelled across the Pacific Ocean at up to 800 kph.
- Two-metre high waves were experienced as far away as Chile, 17,000 km from Japan.

EMERGENCY TEAMS

After a tsunami has passed, emergency teams travel into the disaster zone to help. The teams are made up of different professionals: search and rescue teams, firefighters, doctors, soldiers and relief workers. Volunteers are also often used to search for survivors and help the injured and displaced.

SEARCH AND RESCUE

The main task for search and rescue teams is to dig out survivors trapped under rubble and debris. Sniffer dogs are often brought in to find buried victims. Other teams use boats to rescue people who have been washed out to sea. Many survive this ordeal by clinging on to tsunami wreckage, such as pieces of timber or overturned boats.

FIREFIGHTERS

Fires are often caused by tsunami waves that knock over oil tankers, crack open gas pipes or snap power lines. A small spark can then quickly escalate into a major fire. Firefighters in tsunami-stricken areas face many obstacles. Rubble and debris can prevent a fire engine's access to a fire. Broken water pipes can also prevent firefighters from dousing the flames.

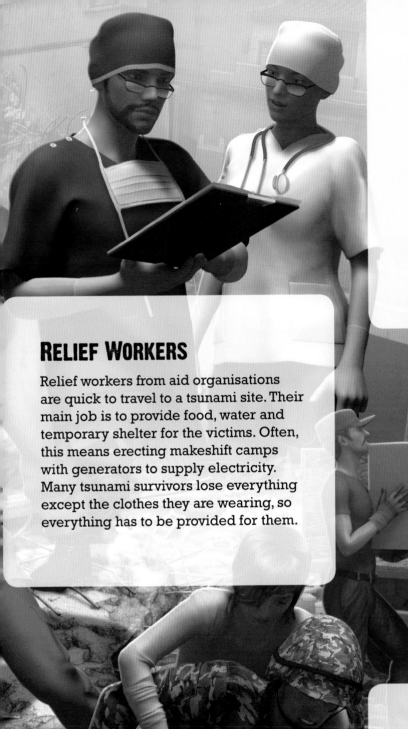

DOCTORS

Many victims need immediate medical help after a tsunami strikes. Often, however, the waves have also damaged or destroyed local hospitals. Sometimes, emergency operations take place in makeshift operating rooms in tents or car parks. Then, long-term health issues have to be addressed, such as vaccinations against disease. Cholera, a disease carried in dirty water, often breaks out after tsunamis.

RELIEF WORKERS

Relief workers from aid organisations are quick to travel to a tsunami site. Their main job is to provide food, water and temporary shelter for the victims. Often, this means erecting makeshift camps with generators to supply electricity. Many tsunami survivors lose everything except the clothes they are wearing, so everything has to be provided for them.

SOLDIERS

Soldiers are sent to tsunami disaster zones to help search for survivors, clear away rubble and deliver supplies. Sometimes, the army is needed to stop people looting homes and businesses. A more gruesome aspect of their work is looking after dead bodies. These have to be buried or cremated quickly before they begin to rot and spread disease.

PREDICTING TSUNAMIS

Tsunamis are destructive forces of nature that no one can prevent. However, unlike an earthquake, there is often time to react to the incoming waves of a tsunami. This is because the waves are formed out at sea and take time to reach the coast. If people are warned, they have a chance to travel to higher ground.

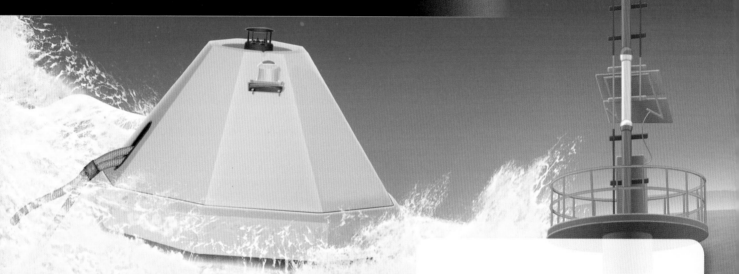

Tsunami Detecting

Tsunami warning centres use sensors to detect tsunamis and communications systems to warn people they are coming.

Seismometers placed on the sea floor can detect undersea earthquakes. Tsunami buoys dotted around the ocean can detect small rises in seawater. Both of these devices then send an alarm via a satellite link to a warning centre. They are very costly to put in place. It would cost around US$20 billion to build a tsunami early warning system in the Indian Ocean.

Tsunami Warning

After a tsunami is detected, coastal residents are quickly warned. In Japan, an early warning system sends out an alert three minutes after a tsunami is detected. The warning is sent out via emergency television and radio broadcasts, alerts to smartphones and social media, and evacuation sirens that are sounded across coastal regions. This early warning system probably saved many lives during Japan's 2011 tsunami (see pages 22–23).

GLOBAL HELP

After the Indian Ocean tsunami of 2004 (see pages 18–19), over 50 countries joined together to form the Global Earth Observation System of Systems (GEOSS). The GEOSS's main job is to link up information from different tsunami warning centres around the world. This means tsunami alerts can go out to potential trouble spots as soon as a tsunami is detected.

Polar-orbiting meteorological satellite

Polar-orbiting earth resources satellite

Geostationary meteorological satellite

High-altitude research aircraft

Radiosonde

Meteorological research aircraft

International aircraft

Automatic weather station

Automated river height and rain gauges

Pilotless aircraft

Meteorological satellite ground station

Voluntary observing ship

Wind profiler

Drifting buoy

Domestic aircraft

Meteorological observing station

PREPARING FOR TSUNAMIS

Tsunami warnings may help save the lives of coastal residents, but only
if they are properly prepared. Preparing communities for a possible
tsunami means building protective walls and evacuation platforms
and educating locals about what signs to look out for.

SEA WALLS

After Japan's devastating 2011 tsunami (see pages 22–23), the government erected
a 125-m-high concrete sea wall along the north-east coast of its main island,
Honshu. The previous sea walls that lined over 40 per cent of Japan's 35,400-km
coastline had offered little protection against the 2011 tsunami.

The coastal regions of other countries devastated by tsunamis often choose to
build reinforced housing on higher ground, rather than new sea walls.

EVACUATION PLATFORMS

Tsunami evacuation platforms are tall towers that people can climb to escape tsunami waves. Around 9 m high, platforms are often built from steel frames with stairs running through the middle. Gaps in the structure provide room for debris-strewn water to pass through.

EDUCATION PROGRAMS

When the 2004 Indian Ocean tsunami struck, many coastal dwellers were not aware what to do, or what to look out for. Today, tsunami education leaflets are produced in many different languages and distributed to villages in tsunami-prone regions. One helpful piece of tsunami information advises people not to go down to the beach after the first wave has passed. Many people do this, mistakenly thinking the danger is over. They are then caught by the second and third waves.

NATURAL WARNINGS

There are two types of tsunami warnings: official and natural. Natural warnings include several tell-tale signs that a tsunami is on its way. These include the sea rapidly receding from the coast, the ground shaking, or a loud roaring sound. When these occur it is time to rush for higher ground immediately, as this tsunami safety brochure advises:

TSUNAMIsafety

Feel a very strong earthquake? **RUN**

See The water withdraw an inusual distance? **RUN**

Hear a strange roar? **RUN**

Roar!

Leave the beach inmediatly if any one of these signs occur and **RUN** to high ground.

High ground may also be a roof, upper floor of a building, or strong tree.

GLOSSARY, BOOKS AND HELPFUL WEBSITES

GLOSSARY

aftershock
A small earthquake which follows the main shock of a large earthquake

asteroid
A flying ball of rock, ranging in size from a car to a planet, which orbits the Sun

catastrophe
A disastrous event which causes great damage and suffering

cholera
A disease caught from infected water which causes vomiting and diarrhoea

debris
Pieces of rubbish and the remains of buildings which are scattered everywhere

displaced
Force someone to leave their home because of a natural disaster

epicentre
The point on Earth's surface directly above an earthquake

evacuation
The ordered removal of people from a place to avoid a disaster

geological
Something which relates to Earth's rocky inner structure

humanitarian crisis
An event which causes widespread human suffering

infrastructure
The basic structures and facilities of a town or city, including roads, buildings, water and power

magnitude
The size or rating of something, such as an earthquake

mantle
The region inside the Earth between the crust and the core

morgue
A building, or a room in a hospital, etc. where dead bodies are kept before they are sent to be buried or burned, sometimes so that they can be examined

nuclear meltdown
The accidental melting of the core of a nuclear reactor resulting in the leakage of dangerous radioactive material

rubble
Broken fragments of rock and brick left behind after the destruction of a building

rupture
The tearing apart of an object

tide
The rise and fall of the sea that happens twice every day

BOOKS

Earthquakes (Nature Unleashed) by Louise and Richard Spilsbury (Franklin Watts, 2018)

Earthquakes (GeoGraphics) by Georgia Amson-Bradshaw (Franklin Watts, 2017)

The Science of Natural Disasters: The Devastating Truth about Volcanoes, Earthquakes and Tsunamis (Science of the Earth) by Alex Woolf (Franklin Watts, 2018)

Tsunamis (Nature Unleashed) by Louise and Richard Spilsbury (Franklin Watts, 2017)

HELPFUL WEBSITES

These websites for kids are all about earthquakes and tsunamis:

https://earthquake.usgs.gov/learn/kids/

http://www.weatherwizkids.com/weather-earthquake.htm

https://www.natgeokids.com/uk/discover/geography/physical-geography/tsunamis/

http://www.sciencekids.co.nz/sciencefacts/earth/tsunamis.html

INDEX

NATURAL DISASTER Z⚡NE

SERIES CONTENT LIST

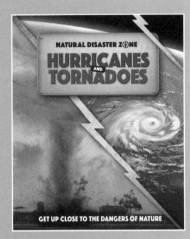

Introducing tornadoes and hurricanes • When a tornado strikes • What's in a tornado? • Tornado winds • Case study: Moore, 2013 • Studying tornadoes • Storm chasers • When a hurricane hits • What makes hurricanes form? • What's in a hurricane? • Categories ofhurricane • Case study: mitch, 1998 • Studying hurricanes • Glossary, books and helpful websites • Index

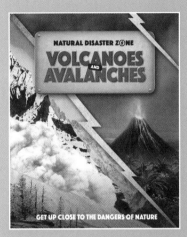

Introducing volcanoes and avalanches • When a volcano erupts • What's in a volcano? • Types of volcanoes • Rock, gas, ash and lava • Case study: Vesuvius, ce 79 • Super volcanoes • People and volcanoes • When an avalanche is released • What's in an avalanche? • Avalanche types • People and avalanches • Case study: Huascaran, 1970 • Glossary, books and helpful websites • Index

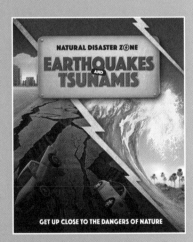

When an earthquake strikes • A word of plates • What's in an earthquake? • Seismic shockwaves • Case study: Kathmandu, 2015 • Predicting earthquakes • When a tsunami strikes • What's in a tsunami? • Case study: Japan, 2011 • Emergency crews • Predicting tsunamis • Preparing for tsunamis • Glossary, books and helpful websites • Index

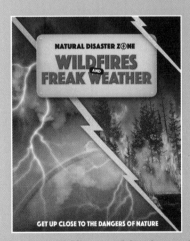

Introducing wildfires and freak weather • When a wildfire ignites • Types of wildfire • Parts of a wildfire • Case study: Victoria, 2009 • Wildfire fighters • Preventing fire • Freak weather • Heatwaves and drought • Flash floods • Ice storms • Dust storms • Fish rain and orange snow • Glossary, books and helpful websites • Index